This Book Belongs To:

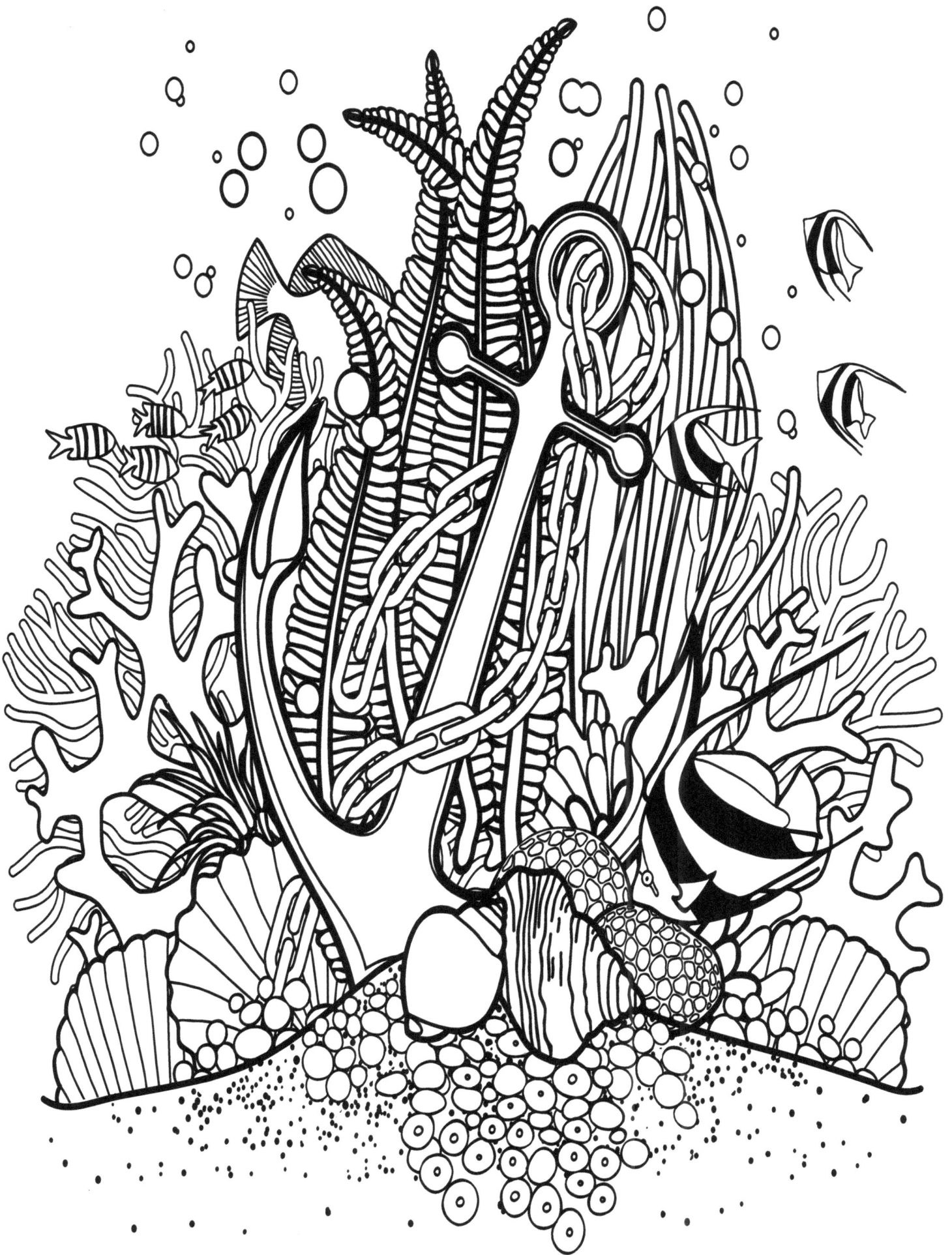

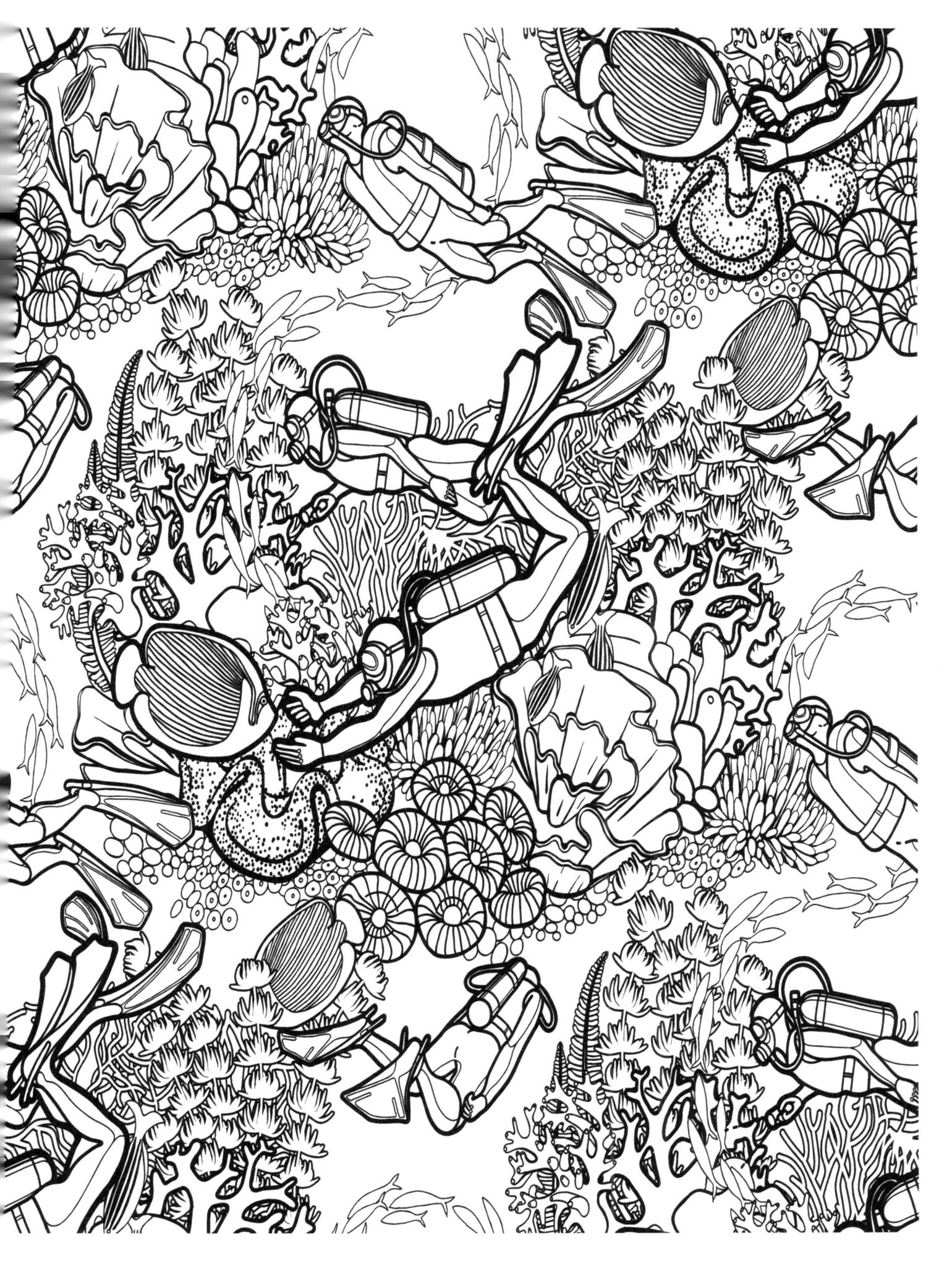

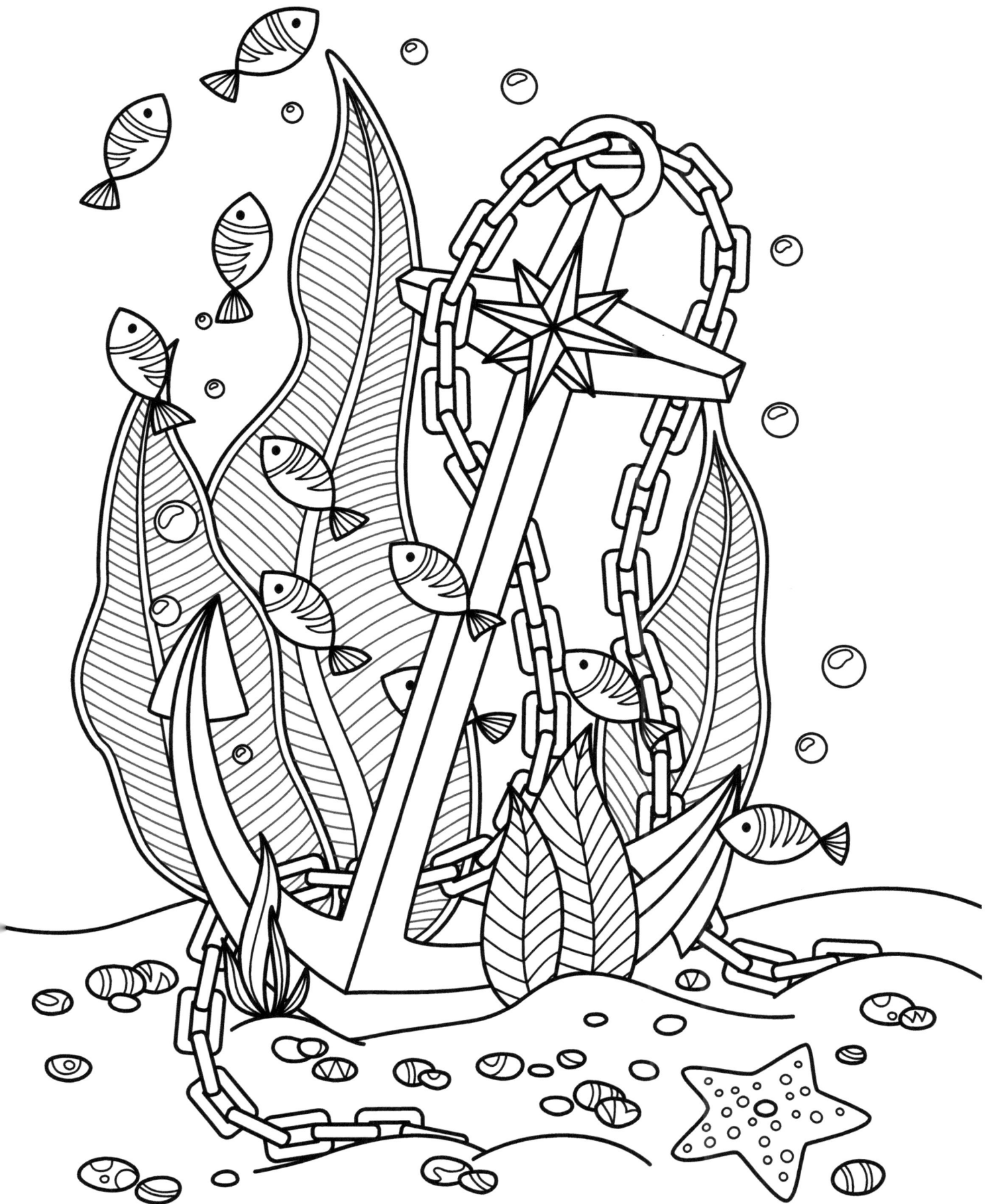

Thank you for your purchase and we hope you enjoyed our book!

Your feedback is greatly appreciated as it lets us know how we are doing!

For all inquiries, email us at groenambrosiapress@gmail.com

Groen

Ambrosia

Press

www.ingramcontent.com/pod-product-compliance
Lightning Source LLC
Chambersburg PA
CBHW080425030426
42335CB00020B/2591